Living Contemplation

Simon Small

Copyright © 2015 Simon Small
All rights reserved

Simon Small asserts the moral right to
be identified as the author of this work

www.simonsmall.info

ISBN-13: 978-1508790488
ISBN-10: 1508790485

CreateSpace Independent Publishing Platform

Also available as a Kindle ebook

Contents

Living Contemplation	1
Remembering the Question	5
The Invitation	8
The Story of Jesus	12
Mind Shock	14
New Thoughts	16
God	18
The Leaf	20
Existing in Existence	21
Shining Stories	22
The Holy Trinity	24
The Peace Conference	26
Knowledge and Belief	28
Contemplation and Suffering	30
The Deep Simplicity of Now	32
The Nicene Creed	34
Love of Humanity	37
Choosing Peace	39
Hubris	42
Heidegger	44
The View from the End of the Road	47
In Memoriam	48
Contemplation and Problems	52
The Impossibility of Peaceful Agitation	55
Where We Stand	56
A Warning	57

The Poetry of Truth	58
Prayer	61
Chess Lessons	62
The Shocking Ordinariness of Death	66
Parable of Dave	70
The Pond	74
The Hummingbird	75
The Possibility of Change	77
Invisible Journey	80
Wind Chimes	81
Bliss	82
Magic and Love	83
Emergence	85
Joy	88
A Baby's Eyes	89

Acknowledgements and Useful Information

Living Contemplation

Living Contemplation

This book is about an ancient strand of the Christian tradition that does not share the lust for certainty that dominates so many modern expressions of the faith.

It is a way of life known as contemplation. It is not for everyone, but speaks powerfully to many in the present age.

It is a way that has been pushed to the edge of Christianity, for it confronts us with the awesome mystery of existence. In the face of this mystery all our certainties fall away and, for some, this is fearful indeed.

It offers a precious gift. Through being ever-more conscious of how much it does not know, it is a path that can live with generosity and openness alongside other insights into the wonder of existence.

Contemplation is the art of paying profound attention to reality, which is to bring our minds completely into the present moment. It is the most intimate expression of prayer.

In contemplation, as we become increasingly aware of the depths of this moment, we see that fundamentally we do not know anything. We see that we live in the midst of breathtaking mystery.

The mystery is unknown because it is beyond thought. It cannot be conceptualised. It is light itself, yet dark to our minds. It has been called the dazzling darkness. But if it is unknown to our minds, a deeper level of who we are knows it intimately, for we are an expression of the Mystery in the world of form. It is us. It is also everything else. And it is more than we can imagine.

On the contemplative path we seek to open to the dazzling darkness that shines in our depths. We sense the presence of a majestic intelligence awaiting our permission to bring us to new birth. It offers to transform our consciousness to reveal a transformed world. The transformation has many names - "metanoia", "awakening", "enlightenment" and "gnosis" are but a few.

For most of us this is a gradual process, for which our minds need conceptual frameworks to give direction and boundaries to the path we tread. But contemplatives never forget that, ultimately, they do not know anything and so hold their ideas of spiritual truth in an open hand, not a closed fist. Ideas and beliefs are seen as open doors beyond which lie new horizons, not barred gates to imprison themselves and others.

In Christianity the mystery, the dazzling darkness, is called "God" and Jesus is its embodiment

For reasons I will never understand, I am a follower of Jesus Christ and a contemplative. All I know is that when I open to his story and commune with him, my heart catches fire. But this is my path and I acknowledge that other stories set other hearts on fire. My experience of the mystery has left no doubt that it speaks in many different ways.

~

A few years ago I wrote a book called *From the Bottom of the Pond*. It was an attempt to share what it is like to live as a Christian contemplative in the midst of the modern world. *From the Bottom of the Pond* is referred to occasionally in this book, as some of the chapters are responses to questions that people raised concerning it.

Living Contemplation is a companion volume. The title has two meanings, both of which are valid. Each book is complete in itself and stands alone. Yet each also supports and deepens the other.

Living Contemplation is a collection of short pieces of writing, of varying style and length, that have emerged over the last ten years. Some have been published previously in magazine articles, blogs and internet forums. Others are from personal writings and are blinking in daylight for the first time. Some editing has been undertaken to harmonise the different styles.

Each chapter is complete in itself. There is no unfolding argument or narrative as the book progresses. It can, therefore, be read in any order or none. Yet although the subjects covered are many and varied, the discerning reader will detect certain recurring themes.

The chapters also have something else in common.

They are all the fruit of contemplative consciousness; that is, thoughts that have surfaced from the depths of a still, prayerful mind, at a particular time of my life. They are not offered as
absolute statements of truth, but as reflections that may be helpful to others. Absolute truth is infinitely beyond any ideas or words, which at their best can only point beyond themselves.

Such writings are of the moment and may sometimes appear inconsistent. This does not matter for they emerged over a long period of time from living contemplation, which always evolves and grows.

Living Contemplation is not a technical manual about how to practice contemplative prayer (or meditation, as many now refer to it). It does not teach how to use a mantra, prayer word, watch the breath, visualise a sacred symbol or any other of the excellent formal techniques for stilling the mind. Those interested in this area might want to explore the teachings of the World Community for Christian Meditation or the Centering Prayer movement.

It is also not specifically a manual on how to live a contemplative life, although much will be discovered anecdotally in the text. There is a wealth of wisdom on this subject to be found in the principles under-pinning the western monastic tradition. A bibliography at the end of the book lists some wonderful modern writers in this area.

Living Contemplation is about what happens when we rise from our place of prayer, go out into the world and, from within a quiet mind, resting in the great mystery, encounter all that is has to offer. It is a collection of experiences, insights and stories that have arisen when I have paid profound attention to each moment.

It suggests that a new world is waiting to be discovered.

There is another book by myself that is occasionally mentioned. *Star Pilgrim* is a novel that explores the contemplative way through the vehicle of mythic fiction. It imagines what might happen to human consciousness and spirituality upon first contact with an alien civilisation; a race of beings for whom the mystery of existence has become the only question that matters.

Remembering the Question

Contemplation is the way that I explore a question.

And in exploring this question, all other questions of meaning are seen in a new light.

My practice of contemplation is formed and shaped by this question and only has meaning in relation to it. I have found that if the question loses focus in my mind, contemplation starts to feel empty and unfulfilling. I have a sense that something has gone wrong, without quite being able to say what has happened. The practice becomes arduous.

More than anything else, it starts to feel abstract and dry.

The question is of a particular kind. It is a question that has no answer, at least in the way we usually understand the term "answer". / It is a question that is so fundamental, so enormous in its implications, that any set of words or concepts that might be offered as an answer would be embarrassed by their inadequacy. Yet to contemplate the question in silence and stillness can have an extraordinary effect upon the mind. The very unanswerable nature of the question seems to cultivate a different experience of consciousness in which, mysteriously, contemplative practice may become contemplation itself.

The question is very simple: "What is this moment?"

This is one form of the universal question that waits patiently for all human beings to look its way. It unites us. It is the question that constantly surrounds us all of the time, but our minds are too full of our lives to see the awesome mystery of life itself. Yet to turn ourselves inside-out and see our lives through the lens of the Mystery, cannot but transform how we live.

If we pause and acknowledge that we truly have no idea what life is, what we are and, even, why anything actually "is" – everything changes. Just reading the last sentence, slowly, may give a sense of what such change tastes like.

So, for me, contemplative practice is first of all to pay profound attention to this moment and to see directly its unfathomable depths. It is to allow its unknown-ness to fill and quieten the mind. Paradoxically, it is to go into a deeper knowing than words and ideas can ever supply. It is to this place (on a good day) that contemplation takes me - often in times of formal practice and, increasingly, spontaneously in the course of daily life.

But because the question has, firstly, taken me into the mystery of the moment where all words must fall away, through Grace I may taste that to which they can only point.

And it is my experience that in this place of waiting, when the mind is very still, one can become aware of an awesome presence and purpose in the depths of the moment. This is why contemplation is prayer. It is an experience of relationship too rich for words.

Indeed, had words and concepts filled the mind the encounter could never have happened so directly. At best, the Presence would have been sensed dimly through their veils or squeezed, terribly misshapen, into their limiting form.

There then comes a time when words, thoughts and the everyday world return and I find myself using the word "God" once more. There is, however, a reticence and hesitation in its use, for in the light of contemplation it seems so inadequate and open to misinterpretation.

And for reasons I do not understand the figure of Jesus becomes ever more central and present. I used to think that I understood who Jesus is, but now that understanding seems no more than useful words written in sand, which at best can only evoke something far too great for them to contain.

The question has become for me a gateway to that which the word "God" points. It awakens me to the truth that now is the only place I ever am and so the only place where God may be known. It is a question that reveals, rather shockingly at first, the extent to which I am usually lost in the world of the mind, dominated by the past and the future. The question awakens me to the truth of now and invites an exploration of its depths. The question gives an awesome setting and a sense of direction to whatever method of contemplative prayer I feel drawn to use, but does not specify the destination. It enables the journey to unfold in its own way.

Also, of course, it is a question that I can carry with me through daily life, gently humming away in the background, from time to time erupting into the forefront of the mind to give a new, vaster perspective on a situation or problem. This is contemplation in action.

To base spiritual practice around questions rather than answers offers another gift that may be particularly needed in the age in which we live. It demonstrates to the world that there is a strand of the Christian tradition that does not share the lust for certainty that can appear to dominate modern expressions of the faith. And through being utterly conscious of the majestic mystery of being, it is a path that can live with generosity and openness alongside other insights into the wonder of existence.

The Invitation

I want to know if you can get up, after the night of grief and despair, weary and bruised to the bone, and do what needs to be done to feed the children.

(ORIAH MOUNTAIN DREAMER: THE INVITATION)

These words are becoming increasingly important to me. They keep popping into my head in response to life experiences.

They were recently given new resonance by the publication of personal writings by Mother Teresa of Calcutta (*Mother Teresa: Come be my Light*). The contents of the book shocked many people. It reveals a Mother Teresa who struggled desperately with a sense of desolation and emptiness during much of her wonderful ministry.

She writes of an incredible longing for God, yet a feeling of not being wanted by God. She says, "Souls hold no attractions. Heaven means nothing – to me it looks like an empty place ...... I dare not utter the words and thoughts that crowd in my heart – and make me suffer untold agony".

The publication of the writings has caused many to doubt her sanctity. Some have even gone so far as to claim that she was a fraud. After all, this is not how it is meant to be. Mother Teresa was supposed to be a great spiritual being, moving through the world in a state of bliss, at one with the peace of God. She was supposed to be an enlightened master, seeing joyfully the face of Jesus in everyone.

But for me, the opposite is the case.

The writings have lifted my admiration for her to new heights. She inspires me even more than she did before. The contrast between her detractors and myself probably arises from a different understanding of the nature of spiritual consciousness.

I have come to see that the flowering of spiritual consciousness has nothing to do with feeling good.

This is an insight that I resisted for a long time. I was dragged to it kicking and screaming. It was not what I wanted to believe.

I began exploring the world's great spiritual teachings (and some not so great) because I was struggling with life. No matter how good things got on the outside, inside there was a great pit of fear and lack of meaning. I thought that the spiritual path offered an end to all of this; that one day I could walk the world experiencing only peace, no matter what was going on around me. And I believed that there were people who were already tasting this. Perfect beings who never knew fear and who's every thought, word and action were perfect.

So my measure of progress on the spiritual path was how good I felt. And, at times, if I was not feeling "good" I struggled to do what needed to be done in the world.

Of course, my experience of life never supported this belief. With increasing frequency I tasted wonderful mystical states and insights, yet periods of inner emptiness still happened. Also, gradually, experience forced me to acknowledge that the "perfect" spiritual beings that inspired me were only human after all. But because I still believed that the spiritual path was about feeling good, I thought that something was wrong with me and with them.

Eventually I became willing to acknowledge the truth rather than pursue an illusion. For me at least, it seems to be part of the natural flow of life that sometimes the sun shines in my mental world, sometimes there are dark clouds and storms, and most of the time there is something in between. Sometimes there seems to be an outer cause of my inner weather, but at other times there is no apparent outer cause.

The great insight for me has been to see that there is nothing wrong with this.

Paradoxically, I am now truly at peace because I accept lack of peace when it occurs.

This is not denial or dissociation. It is looking fully into the emptiness and accepting it. It is contemplation – paying loving attention to what is.

Strangely, I am finding that as I accept the mind in whatever state it happens to be, there is often an inner expansion. There is an experience of being the sky through which the mind weather passes in its fleeting existence, rather than of being the weather itself. It is an exhilarating new sense of identity, but one that has no name or history. This is a state that, previously, I usually only tasted in the depths of meditation or the beauty of nature - and found frustratingly difficult to take into the everyday world. It is a state that embraces feelings (good or bad), but from a transcendent place.

And in this expanded state something else happens. I seem to hear more clearly a quiet, wordless voice that has been speaking to me for aeons. I hear it now more frequently, not only in the stillness of prayer but walking the streets of daily life.

There has also been a profound change of perspective.

My emotional weather seems less important.

So I am in awe of Mother Teresa. She seems to have experienced a perpetual mind hurricane for a large part of her life. Yet she could still, "… get up, after the night of grief and despair, weary and bruised to the bone, and do what needs to be done to feed the children".

This is a different kind of spirituality to what I am used to, but one by which I am inspired. It is a spirituality of pure faith.

I don't know why her experience of inner desolation

was so intense and long lasting, whereas mine always seems passing. Perhaps if I lived as she did, surrounded by such suffering, it would be that way for me too.

And could I have got up and fed the children for fifty years feeling as she did?

The Story of Jesus

As Christmas approaches, I am once more being reminded of the incredible power of the story of Jesus.

I am currently reading the *Gospel of Luke* at the leisurely rate of a few verses a day and am noticing the effect it is having on me.

It is difficult to put into words, but I am aware that in the midst of daily life there are occasions when I see things differently to what would otherwise have been the case. I have particularly noticed that I seem at the moment to be a little more forgiving of others and have a genuine desire to see beyond the surface. I have also noticed – and this is truly extraordinary – that I am enjoying the Christmas season and finding real meaning in it. This has not happened since I was a small child. My family have also noticed this and, being very familiar with my usual scrooge-like grumpy state at this time of year, are astonished at the transformation.

Although I cannot be sure, I think that the Gospel is affecting me because I am reading it in a particular way. I have turned-off all my analytic/sceptical/critical tendencies and am simply allowing myself to become absorbed in the story.

I am not concerning myself with whether the text is historically accurate or if Jesus actually physically healed people, calmed storms, cast out demons, rose from the dead, etc, etc. Such questions matter to me less and less now – not least because they are ultimately unanswerable. I also find the disputes that inevitably arise around such questions arid and soul-draining

I am now dissolving into the story and allowing it to live in my depths unhindered. And in those depths, in ways that I cannot pin down, it is encountering the hidden threads of my own story and nurturing subtle changes in perception and desire, that are then seeping mysteriously back to the surface.

This is to relate to the story of Jesus as myth – in the true meaning of the word. That is, a story which has enfolded within it deep meanings and insights that, as we live the story, find their way past our discriminating consciousness into the subterranean currents of the mind. The mythic story transforms us from the inside outwards, in ways that are impossible to identify.

And in being so transformed, we are opened to the divine reality to which the story of Jesus points and evokes with awesome power.

Mind Shock

I am starting to be shocked by my own mind.

I am starting to be shocked by the sheer intensity of the story that is constantly running. It is like a hurricane that never loses energy. It is a story that is out of control and seems never-ending.

It is the story of Simon Small. It is the story of his fears, desires, hopes and emotions, which is being constantly re-written by the imaginings of past and future. It is the story through which he reacts to the outside world, which in turn triggers yet more highly energised fears, desires, hopes and emotions.

Of course, if I can see the story, what I truly am cannot be the story. I must be the story-teller, who for so long has been lost in story-telling that he has forgotten about the real world. This is easy when everyone else is doing the same. Indeed, all of our stories are inter-twined, constantly battling with each other for supremacy.

I have seen this for some time, but only now, as my vision clears further, am I beginning to see the extreme, frightening intensity of the story. As the deeper part of who I am rests in stillness, in contemplative consciousness, it watches the strand of itself that is still absorbed in the story with increasing horror. I am realising that part of me is mad. It is insane. This is shocking.

What is even more shocking is that I am aware that something in me remains profoundly drawn to losing itself in the story.

Something inside prefers the madness, even though, like a drug addict, it knows that on that path lies only suffering. In some unconscious way I must still believe that it is my friend.

But although shocked by what I see, the same quality of seeing brings with it another realisation.

There is also something drawing me out of the madness. There is a presence in my mind that is not of the story, which is leading me to higher ground. As I see the incredible, intoxicating intensity of the story it is clear that on my own this liberation would never be possible.

Something or someone is trying to gently wake me up.

New Thoughts

There is a spiritual teaching that claims our minds see only the past.

As I have paid profound attention to my own mind, I have seen that this is true. It is very rare that I have a new thought.

Most of the time my mind is putting a new mask on old thoughts. I see the present moment through the many veils of what I think I know. Even when I imagine the future, it is the past projected in some way. My mind goes around in circles, repeating the old.

I have realised that it is an essential spiritual practice to regularly have new thoughts. Every day, if possible.

By this I do not mean a thought that is the continuation of previous thinking, a variation on an old theme, but something beautifully new and different, that seems to just appear in the mind, as if from nowhere.

It's easy to tell the difference.

A new thought is like a bomb going off somewhere in the mind. We have no doubt when it happens. A new thought leaves behind an inner glow, a quiet sense of bliss. We feel more alive.

We cannot force new thoughts, but an invitation from a quiet mind will always, sooner or later, bring a response. Probably sooner.

New thoughts must not, however, be grasped too tightly, but allowed to evolve and move on. Otherwise they freeze into the repetitive mind and become old thoughts, drained of life, nothing but dead memory.

God

It is impossible for the human mind to conceive of anything that does not have a cause.

All it can grasp is a never-ending sequence of cause and effect, beginnings and endings. This perception creates time and space.

So when thought contemplates the universe it inevitably assumes that it must have had a moment of beginning. It can only think in terms of time and space. Indeed, in these terms there must have been a beginning, but in the realm of timelessness "beginnings" have no meaning.

The source of everything that we experience must include within itself all that the human mind can be. It must also be possible, if not probable, that it contains far more than even this; perhaps infinitely more.

The source of all that is, the causeless cause, must therefore include personhood. God is a person.

God is also infinitely more.

We do not understand what a person is. We do not understand what it is to be "individual", but we think that we do and so construct an idea of God in the image of what we believe we are.

Our contemplative pilgrimage is to reverse this path; to repent. It is to turn ourselves inside-out and allow God to construct us in the truth of what it is to be a person.

God is revealed in many ways. He is revealed through the great religious writings, through creation itself and through the response to prayer both now and down the ages.

But there is another source of revelation. Human beings can be a revelation of God. It is in God's image that we are created. To understand what it is to be human is to go deeper into the nature of God.

The Leaf

I watched a leaf fall to the ground today. I watched as it fluttered through the air for a few seconds and then watched as it came gently to ground. One moment it was flying gaily, full of life. The next it was just lying there, dead still among thousands of other leaves.

My mind could not take in the gone-ness of the transformation. That unique moment of transfixing, whirling, reflecting flight would never be again. It was gone forever.

I was shocked by the power of the experience. In those few moments I had seen the truth of life in the raw. It was shocking because I had seen the raw truth about myself and all that exists. It was shocking because I had seen the truth, not an idea about the truth. The truth was there in front of me, before thought began. I became the truth. It was direct realisation.

My mind could not take in the gone-ness of the leaf because I struggle to take in my own gone-ness; that the Sun will rise on a day when I am not. I know this as an idea and can accept it at that level. But the direct, naked truth of my gone-ness, that the leaf evoked, shook something deep inside.

It was an autumn moment, full of melancholy and beauty. I am deeply grateful, for after the shock has come profound peace. It is the truth that sets us free.

Existing in Existence

Human beings are conditioned to focus only on that which exists. It is a rare human being who contemplates existence itself.

Yet that which exists is always only temporary, transient and impermanent. Everything that "only" exists, whether it be a planet, a human being, an amoeba or a lump of rock, is born and dies, arises and ceases. All is falling away in every moment. It is only existence itself that is eternal; is not born and does not die; does not arise or cease.

The religious quest, which is the search for ultimate truth, is to become at one with existence, not with that which merely exists. It is to relate to being itself, not to become attached to, or venerate, or seek salvation in, temporary manifestations of being.

Human beings are manifestations of this sea of existence. We arise like small waves, reach our peak and then dissolve back into the surging foam. But we have been given a great gift, which is ours to express if we so choose.

The gift is conscious union with existence itself.

To take our existing into communion with existence. This is the religious path. The very meaning of the word "religion" is to "rejoin".

In the Christian tradition this is termed "salvation".

Shining Stories

Last week I watched a television programme about the atom. I was fascinated by the story of its discovery and of the incredibly strange sub-atomic world that theoretical physics has revealed. In fact, I was more than fascinated. I was inspired. The story left an afterglow that lasted several days. As I write these words it is starting to return.

I am noticing increasingly how some stories have this effect on me. They seem to awaken something inside. They set the heart on fire. A light seems to shine from the stories, which connects me with the mystery of being. That evokes the experience of love.

Such stories need not be "true" to have this effect. The story I encountered about the sub-atomic world is certainly far from being the complete truth. It is an unseen world, revealed through imagination and mathematics, and our picture of it is most certainly incomplete and inaccurate.

Indeed, this may well be part of the reason that such stories are so powerful. They are humble stories that make no claim to completeness or certainty. They reflect the vastness of our unknowing in this sea of existence.

They remind us of Sir Isaac Newton when said he felt "like a boy playing on the seashore …. finding a smoother pebble or prettier shell …. whilst the great ocean of truth lay all undiscovered before me".

There is one story that affects me in this way like no other. I do not know why this is. I have tried in the past to turn my back on the story, but its power is too strong. It shines for me with such a pure light that it brings tears to my eyes. It is the story of that mysterious figure we know as Jesus Christ.

In historical terms, I know little about him – even to the point where I cannot be sure that he ever walked the Earth. Yet, for reasons I do not understand, to hear his story and to commune with him evokes a sense of presence that fills my heart. I can genuinely appreciate other great spiritual figures, whose words and lives also shine, but they do not have the same effect on me. I do not know why this is and fully accept that for others the reverse is true. This is part of the Mystery.

Perhaps they are just on another part of the seashore being entranced by other pebbles and shells. Perhaps this is how it is meant to be, so that together we can see and love more.

In the practice of contemplation we give profound attention to the present moment and, in so doing, see the path that links each moment. I am realising that an important element of this practice is to notice the stories that shine and, conversely, those that leave in their wake only dullness.

In the former we find stepping-stones that lead us into the Mystery of God.

The Holy Trinity

"As above so below, except after another fashion", claims the ancient hermetic axiom.
    Or to put it another way, in the creation the nature of the creator is reflected.
    To those who pay profound attention, this moment is one and it is many. This is self-evident.
    This moment has always been, has no gaps, no boundaries, is fathomless and is utterly still. It is an unblemished and unlimited field of eternal being.
    Yet like waves on an ocean, the many arise from the one in glorious, mind-blowing variety, each expression encapsulating the essence of the one. The many and the one, present, now, with no separation.
    The universe is a unity - the clue is in the name. Yet look at the night sky, life on Earth, down a microscope or imagine the sub-atomic world.
    Or look at our own minds. A single field of consciousness, yet in the same moment a cornucopia of thoughts.
    There is one God; Father, Son and Holy Spirit. God is one and God is three.
    The doctrine of the Trinity is difficult for many Christians. It makes no rational sense. How can something be one and three at the same time?

Or to put it another way, how can something be one and many at the same time. Perhaps the clues are all around us, if we pay attention.

Some words from the Gospel of Thomas:

> *Jesus said, "If they ask you,*
> *'What is the sign of your father within you?'*
> *say to them, 'It is movement and rest.'"*

The Peace Conference

I was once invited to lead a seminar at an important church conference devoted to world peace.

Some of the main speakers were well-known faces from television. I have no idea why I was invited. I was unknown and had never worked in this field. I suspect the invitation was a mistake and that I should have declined, but it seemed interesting. I had never been to a conference devoted to peace.

So we gathered to debate the Middle East, the work of the United Nations, the role of the church in places of conflict and other weighty topics - about which I knew very little.

This should have been a problem, but I had come up with a cunning plan. Instead of peace in the world, I would talk about inner peace, in our own hearts.

I had only been at the conference for a few minutes when I realised what a radical and subversive plan this might turn out to be.

I was approached through the milling crowd of peace devotees by someone I knew. They were really angry with me. Previously, in connection with another matter, I had politely disagreed about a proposed course of action.

Upon spotting me, they immediately embarked on a second attempt to change my mind. This also failed and they stormed-off into the peace conference.

It was not a good start.

With a deep breath, I went into the main hall and listened to the famous speakers on the subject of world peace.

They were erudite, reasoned and powerful. The questions from the audience were intelligent and searching. All genuinely wanted the best for the world.

I noticed two things, however.

First, I'd heard it all before. The same things had been said, in some form, by previous generations. Nothing seemed to have changed over all the years. The world did not seem any more peaceful.

Einstein's famous dictum "the consciousness that creates a problem cannot solve it" kept playing in the back of my mind.

I noticed something else. So many people at the peace conference were angry.

They were angry with politicians, with particular countries, with the United Nations, with global corporations and a host of other entities. They were even angry with other peace activists who disagreed with them about the best way forward. Sometimes the anger was out in the open, more often simmering just below the surface, barely contained. The Chair had to work hard at times to keep control of proceedings.

Einstein's words came into my mind once more.

In fairness, perhaps they would have said that they were not angry, but passionate. But I am suspicious of euphemisms. I am also wary of passion - too often it is blind.

It was a relief when the main conference broke-up into small seminars around particular topics. Participants could choose which to attend, based on their interests.

My seminar on inner peace did not attract many people, but I think the few that came appreciated it.

I wonder if it is possible to share what we do not have?

Knowledge and Belief

I sometimes have conversations with people who say that religion is not for them.
"It's alright for you", they say, "You can just believe, but I'm incapable of that. I need proof. I need to see something; touch something. I can't just believe".
They are usually surprised when I say that I am also not interested in just believing; that I, too, am not capable of that. I want to know.
I tell them that my religion is experiential. I am religious because of experience and explore religion (and other disciplines) to understand those experiences.
It is the experiences that nurture a growing sense of both belief and knowing.
Very often they come back with the riposte, "Ah, yes, well it's O.K. for you, but I've never had such experiences. Perhaps if I saw a miracle or sign of some kind, I might be able to 'know' like you claim to".
I have a simple and obvious reply. I direct their attention to what is before their face.
"But you have experienced a miracle", I say.
"No I haven't", they reply, often indignantly.
"But you're in the middle of one; and it is in you. In fact, it is you".
They usually look puzzled at this point, so I offer some

explanation.

The very fact that we exist is a miracle.

The very fact that there is anything, at all, is a miracle.

The universe does not have to exist. This strange blue ball floating in space that we call home does not have to exist. This room does not have to exist. We do not have to exist. There does not have to be anything at all.

There could just be void, yet for some reason there is existence.

What greater sign, what greater miracle does anyone need?

To take it further, there is order in existence. It isn't random. There is evolution, there is birth and death, there is change and there are laws.

Does not such order strongly suggest a foundation in a mind; what else do we know that imposes order? And is it not the nature of mind to express intention, meaning and purpose?

Yet it must be a mind so awesome as to be almost incomprehensible to us.

If we wanted, we could use the word "God" to describe such an all-pervading presence.

Then I add one more idea.

Could it be that our minds are but sparks of that one majestic mind and that by moving our attention inwards, into our still depths, we might eventually taste its presence?

Could it be that this is the deepest prayer?

Sometimes, but not always, people walk away thoughtfully after such conversations.

From the Gospel of Thomas:

> *Jesus said, "Know what is before your face*
> *and that which is hidden will be revealed.*
> *For there is nothing hidden which will*
> *not be revealed."*

Contemplation and Suffering

In response to *From the Bottom of the Pond*, people have sometimes raised an objection to the contemplative way.

It is usually along the lines of, "This inner path sounds so selfish. Should not our prayer and action be a response to the suffering of the world, not seeking our own bliss?"

My first, and fundamental, response to this objection is to say that contemplation is a calling from God. It is not for everyone.

Early in the book, I emphasise that the spiritual life is a response to Grace. We do not decide what it is we are to do, but seek to discern what we are being asked to do. This requires humility and an acceptance of the Mystery of God.

For some this calling will involve an active outer life, for others more of an inner journey. And the balance can change over a lifetime (as it has with me).

Many of us have experienced moments when something within responds to a conversation or book and we know that we must explore this further.

From the Bottom of the Pond was written to evoke this realisation in those for whom contemplation is the way. At this time in our culture I believe that this is the case for many.

Also, in the chapter entitled *Three-fold Prayer*, I talk about how contemplation lives alongside, and in harmony with, other forms of prayer (including those that hold the suffering of the world before God). The balance will differ between individuals according to their calling. Part of the plea of the book (chapter nine) is for people to accept this difference.

A contemplative has no choice as to what they are.

And contemplation is not an easy path. You get to spend a lot of time with your mind and this will be on occasion a very difficult experience (see the chapter entitled *The Rocky Path of Contemplation*).

Chapter thirteen was meant to illustrate that contemplation is not divorced from the problems of the world, but enables us to see and relate to the world in a deeper way. Inner stillness enhances outer vision. Any action rooted in such vision will be far more effective and loving. I say in this chapter that the more we are still inwardly, the more we see through the eyes of God.

What better foundation for action in the world could there be?

The Deep Simplicity of Now

Have you noticed how simple this moment is?
And, paradoxically, have you also noticed its unfathomable depth and awesome mystery?
This is the shift in consciousness to which the word "contemplation" refers.
Spiritual teachings, ancient and modern, can only be understood from within this quality of awareness. They then become a humble description of a living experience and a collection of tentative ideas that always point beyond themselves. Such teachings possess a sense of simplicity and yet, also, astonishing richness.
Teachings that do not come alive in the stillness of now, that retain a feeling of complexity and of time, should be gently discarded.
The Mystery of Existence is not complex, it is deep.
Time is complex; this moment is clear and whole.
In an age when spiritual seekers are bombarded with an unending stream of teachings, it is the simplicity and mystery of this moment that will show the way; that will grant discernment.
I write these words because over many years I have led seminars, given talks and listened to a lot of people. I have been left with an overwhelming impression of so many being lost in complexity, time and thought.

I have tried to explain that what they seek is not to be found in the future, in yet more ideas, but by seeing what is before their face.

But it is very difficult for minds immersed in the complex to grasp the simple.

The Nicene Creed

A significant number of ordinary Christians have a problem reciting the Nicene Creed in church on a Sunday morning.

In my role as a spiritual director, it is a subject that is often raised for discussion. Most seem to have problems with particular bits of the text. A few with most of it. It is common for people to have struggled on in silence for years.

My response is usually along the following lines.

First, something very practical.

We have to accept that this creed will always be at the heart of the Church and of the liturgy, no matter what we may think of it. I have frequently heard the view expressed that it should be adapted or moved to a less prominent position in the service. Two thousand years of tradition, across all the main denominations, is never going to be discarded. Neither should it be. It has played a crucial part in holding us together over all this time.

So, if we are struggling, we have to find a way to live with it in generosity. To say the words through clenched teeth will do no one any good. More than that, we need to consider the possibility that, by relating to the words in a new way, we may find hidden depths. Perhaps there is a great gift that we are missing.

I then offer the following, which is based on my own experience.

It can be helpful to reflect on our relationship with the creed over time. When I have done this it has become apparent that the relationship has not been static, but has subtly evolved. Something I struggled with a few years ago, now seems inspiring. A line I used to have no problem with, is now a challenge. It is a living relationship, that I can now see has been working away below the surface over a long period. The words seem to be changing me from the inside out, while I am busy doing other things.

I suspect the problem most people have is that for a long time they simply said the words by rote, caught-up in the wider liturgical atmosphere. Then they started thinking about their meaning and intellectually rebelled. My experience seems to suggest that this is a natural and necessary process that, eventually, takes us to a deeper place, beyond rationalising, where the words come alive in a new way.

This evolution suggests that something beyond the words, far beyond their literal meaning, is reaching out through them.

Then there is the contemplative dimension.

Words and their meanings matter - but only up to a certain point. I am aware of the literal meaning of the creed, which is essential, but this is set against the vast mystery that permeates and surrounds the words. More than anything else, it has been the quiet growth of this sense of mystery that seems to have brought a peace with the words.

Perhaps this sense of the deep, vibrant unknown allows the words to be seen from another, less worldly perspective. From contemplative consciousness the words come alive as mythic poetry.

The Nicene Creed is most certainly the product of a sordid political process in the early church, and has been much misused since, but I have no doubt that God is at its heart nevertheless.

When I say the creed now, I relate to it as part of the rhythm of the whole liturgy, which is gradually opening my consciousness (and those around me) to the presence of the numinous. For this to work, I have to let go into the journey, without holding back.

I am also uplifted by being able to join with a group of disparate people in seeking God - even if we would each understand the words we say a little differently. This is a beautiful thing.

Love of Humanity

I used to think that, apart from certain individuals, I could not love humanity.

When I walked down the street, watched the news on television or listened to the shouting outside my house on a Friday night, I despaired of people in general. Even ordinary conversations often left me depressed at the shallowness of so many people's lives.

I felt something must be wrong with me. After all, I was a "spiritual person", a priest even. I was supposed to love everyone. I would comfort myself with the argument that religion was about God, not other people, but this ruse never really satisfied.

I did not love, as I was called to do as a Christian.

I remember several times asking Jesus to teach me how to love, but seemingly without getting a response.

It was Julian of Norwich, a great Christian mystic of the fourteenth century, who one day showed me that there was nothing to learn; that I already loved humanity desperately.

One morning I was reading her *Revelations of Divine Love* as part of my prayer time. She was speaking about the terrible pain of Mary at seeing her son, Jesus, on the Cross. Julian commented that Mary could only hurt so much because she loved so much. If she had not loved there would have been no pain.

This was not an idea that was new to me, but that morning, almost certainly because my mind was very still, in a profound state of contemplative consciousness, it went very deep. And in doing so, it triggered another insight that showed me that I had never been out of love with my brothers and sisters.

I saw that the logic could be reversed. If I felt pain at the suffering of others, I must love them.

In the stillness, my mind then recalled the difficulty I had watching suffering on the television, whether it be people in the midst of a natural disaster, criminals being set upon by a mob (no matter how "deserving") or simply someone being embarrassed.

I felt their pain. It scrunched me up inside.

If I felt their pain, I must love them. I had always loved them.

In that moment, I laid down a great burden.

Choosing Peace

A great spiritual teacher once told me something that I have been trying to work with ever since.

He said that in difficult situations, no matter how pressing matters seemed to be, whatever emotions were at work, the only important thing was to bring peace to the mind.

He claimed that as the mind found stillness, answers would come. He also suggested that, very often, reality itself would respond in remarkable and mysterious ways.

Of course, in the stresses and intensity of life, this is not easy to do. We become absorbed in the drama and the mind fills with chains of thought, often incomplete and semi-coherent. We may still believe that to bring peace to the mind is a good thing – but only after we've sorted out the problem at hand. It feels too urgent and all-consuming.

This teaching came to my rescue a few years ago with regard to a particular situation. Unlike so many other occasions, I finally remembered to apply it. The results were extraordinary.

I live in Glastonbury. It is an old market town, not designed with the motor car in mind. Parking is a real problem. At that time, I had to leave my car on the road in a small designated parking bay. If the bay was full, I had to park quite a distance away. Having got a space outside my house, I was always reluctant to give it up without good reason.

The problem was that the Police would close the parking bay whenever there was a public event in the town, claiming that it eased traffic flow.

One Saturday I knew that there was a big event in Glastonbury, so was expecting a knock on the door from the Police, accompanied by an instruction to move my car somewhere else. From the moment I got out of bed, I became increasingly angry at the prospect. I decided to refuse to move the car and persuade my neighbours to do the same, on the basis that the police instruction was not lawful. My mind was whirling ever faster as it kept rehearsing what I would say. It continued as I went for a shower, becoming increasingly frenetic.

Suddenly, I couldn't stand my mind any more. I knew that I had become lost in a kind of madness.

Then the words of the teacher popped into consciousness and, in my desperation, I made a real effort to calm my thoughts. Almost immediately, out of the blue, a question appeared in my mind; "What would peace do here?"

As soon as the question arose, my mind became very still and started to ponder possible answers. I quickly saw what peace would do – it would simply move the car to another location and then get on with life in a state of equanimity. It was so obvious. My mind became even more still and then another thought appeared – "Would I be allowed to park at the retreat house a little way down the road?"

I'd not had much contact with the retreat house up to that point, having met the warden only once, very briefly. Yet in the stillness I knew that I should go and ask. So I walked down the road and knocked on the door. I was greeted with a big smile.

"Simon", the warden said, "It's really good to see you. Come on in".

She immediately agreed to my request to leave my car in the car park and even said that my neighbours could do so as well. She then started talking about the retreat house and asked if I would lead some events there, and also asked if she could sell my books. By the time I left half an hour later, all kinds of new openings had appeared.

More was to follow.

A short time later I was invited to become the chaplain at the retreat house and now live there.

It was one of those almost dream-like experiences, where you just watch everything flowing. It's difficult to convey the sense of power that came with it. Not only did my mind become a beautiful place to be, inspiration flowered and the world responded in an extraordinary way.

All because I chose peace instead of my imagined grievance.

Hubris

Human beings have an almost overwhelming impulse to see themselves as the centre of existence.

Everything is then viewed and interpreted from this place. So distortion, ignorance and falsehood enter into human life, with all the suffering that this inevitably brings. The greatest questions and the deepest insights are hammered into mutant shapes in order to fit into the human soap opera – playing itself out on a tiny speck of dust, orbiting an insignificant sun in an unfathomably immense, multi-dimensional universe.

The world's greatest religions and spiritual teachings are not immune from this disease. This seems extraordinary, given that they claim insight into the most profound questions about the human condition.

But perhaps it is not surprising given the struggle that my own tradition experienced in merely accepting that the Earth orbited the sun, rather than the reverse; an apt metaphor for a greater malaise.

The antidote to this original sin has two ingredients.

The first is contemplative prayer.

Through the sustained practice of stilling the mind and bringing our attention into the present, gradually the illusory nature of our habitual way of perceiving reality is revealed. Once revealed, it is laid aside naturally. Our spiritual teachings come alive in a new way, often as though we have never encountered them before. What seemed so familiar, now seems new. That to which the word "God" points is now glimpsed. Jesus is met afresh – as both an earthly and a meta-cosmic being.

We are filled with the awesome mystery of existence.

This is what I try to describe and evoke in *From the Bottom of the Pond*.

The second ingredient is imagination.

Standing on this small speck of dust, in a tiny corner of this vast universe, living mundane lives, it is hard to see from the other end of the telescope. But we have been given the greatest of gifts. We have minds that can picture new, extraordinary possibilities. And in so doing our consciousness is transformed. This is why imagination can become prayer. It opens us to the unspeakable majesty of God.

This is what I try to do in *Star Pilgrim*.

Heidegger

Sometimes I cannot resist a bit of name-dropping. So here goes. I am currently reading a book called *Introduction to Metaphysics* by Martin Heidegger, a famous twentieth century philosopher. This sounds impressive, but in all honesty I have yet to finish the first chapter. It's hard going. Perhaps it's a bad translation. Or more likely it's a result of the endemic inability of most western philosophers to communicate with anything approaching clarity. I have a suspicion that I will soon give up and move on to something more digestible.

But this would be a pity, as I sense beneath the verbal concrete lies something of incalculable value. This is because the book starts with the greatest question there is.

"Why are there beings at all instead of nothing?"

I bought a copy of the book when someone told me that it started with this question. The discovery of this question, albeit in a slightly different form, was one of the great turning points of my life. It was the moment that a great confusion ended and clarity was suddenly present – not because I had found an answer, but because I had finally discovered the question that mattered. It was the question that had always been present, but dissolved in my unconscious, hovering at the edge of awareness like a name or date that you cannot quite remember.

I was at my computer preparing for a meeting I would

be leading that evening exploring a particular spiritual teaching. I was getting frustrated as nothing I could think of seemed to hit the mark. But, also, I did not know what mark it was that I was trying to hit. Then, for no obvious reason, a question erupted into my mind and changed everything.

"Why is there anything? Why isn't there just nothing, an unimaginable void?"

This was followed by a simple statement as I looked around the room. "None of this has to be".

These questions and insights were not abstract. They came from the gut. They filled me. And they made the whole world look utterly different. They stopped my mind in its tracks and silenced the usual chatter. All that was left was an experience of complete, awesome mystery.

In the intensity of the moment, I did not want to lead the group that evening. All the spiritual philosophy and practices suddenly felt irrelevant; maybe even part of the confusion that I'd been experiencing. Staring me in the face was the fundamental, world-shattering question that demanded all of my attention.

Interestingly, I once heard a speaker suggest that all further human enquiry should stop until Heidegger's question had been answered, because nothing solid could be built until the foundation was in place.

As the power of the moment lessened, however, I began to see that spiritual teachings (and all other expressions of human knowledge) did still matter, but they could only be seen truly when set against the vastness of the greatest question. It must be the backdrop, the context for all that we do. Its natural fruit will always be humility and true openness. It destroys any sense of control that we may have. It makes us aware that we have no idea what we are a part of.

Most importantly, the question opens us to relationship with what lies at the heart of the mystery.

It has been suggested that western philosophy has, perhaps unconsciously, avoided this question for millennia. It is too big, too fearful and apparently unanswerable. It undermines the very reason for a philosopher to get out of bed in the morning.

I would suggest that this criticism could also be applied to most of the world's spiritual seekers. We immerse ourselves in all kinds of theologies, philosophies, practices and communities, while ignoring the elephant in the room that stands right in front of our noses. Once it is acknowledged, any sense of our own power has to be abandoned.

It is only in the abandonment of our illusory sense of power that something new can happen – something that emerges into our now purified minds to re-energize a relationship that was always present, but lost beneath all the confusion.

The View From the End of the Road

I sometimes imagine that I am on my death bed, looking back over my life.

I do it as an act of prayer.

The effect can be extraordinary. The seeming complications generated by my usual immersion in life often acquire a simple clarity.

I have particularly noticed that the relentless inner pressure for financial and other security fades and questions around love, creativity, growth and authenticity come to the fore.

The imaginative act of remembering my inevitable death takes me into a new consciousness, wherein the challenges of life are seen against an infinitely greater backdrop.

Of course, the great task is to keep this expanded perspective once the exercise is over. But it always leaves an after-glow, a sense of having touched deep truth.

In Memoriam

I recently read a book in which a man talked about the spiritual teachers who had helped him. Some were famous, others obscure. Around the same time I discovered that a great spiritual teacher of my own had died. I will call him George.

It was not obvious that George was a great spiritual teacher. In fact, one could have easily gained the opposite impression. This was certainly not an accolade that he would have applied to himself. George's life was a disaster area in ways too numerous to mention. He blundered from one crisis to another, often seeking escape from his worries in unwise and damaging ways.

His social skills could also be lacking. At times this could be amusing. I remember him attending a public talk I did many years ago on some spiritual topic. It was a small, intimate room, which was soon a focus of intense concentration. At that point, George produced a packet of very crunchy potato chips that he proceeded to eat with gusto, very noisily. I think that it is fair to say that the atmosphere was broken and never really recovered for the rest of the evening. Looking back now, it is very funny. That was not how I felt at the time.

In fact, I think it is fair to say that it would be difficult to imagine anyone further from the usual image of a spiritual teacher than George. Were he here as I write these words, he would be nodding his head vigorously in agreement and laughing in the way only he could.

Yet it is George, this apparently most unlikely source, who was midwife to a couple of the most significant turning points of my spiritual journey.

The first such moment occurred one afternoon as I was reading a book on Buddhism. I had come across a chapter on the Theravada tradition. It was one of those moments when you know something has entered your life that is going to be important. I had struggled to relate to Buddhism up to that point, but the chapter had awoken something. I remember putting the book down and pondering how to find out more about Theravada. Then there was a knock on the door.

There stood George. I must admit that my heart sank a little. He could sometimes require great patience. I inwardly took a deep breath and invited him in, but he declined and simply held out an old plastic shopping bag. George owned a second-hand bookshop and had that day acquired some new stock, which included multiple copies of some titles.

"I had a feeling that you might find these interesting," he said holding out the bag. "Don't worry, I've got lots of copies", he added as he moved off.

I took the bag inside and closed the door. What was in the bag changed my life. It was a set of books about Theravada Buddhism.

The second moment of George-inspired inspiration occurred one evening at a discussion group I was leading. Fortunately, on this occasion he had not brought his packet of potato chips. The topic for the evening was "Extra-ordinary Experiences". I invited people to share any experiences they had encountered that seemed to defy conventional explanation. As is nearly always the case in such discussions, people were at first slightly sheepish, but then began to open up with all kinds of odd happenings – pre-cognitive dreams, visions, and particularly glimpses of, and conversations with dead relatives. I have learned down the years that most people have had strange experiences, but few talk about them. Many push them down in the mind to a place where they can no longer disturb consciousness.

The evening was going well, I thought, until George, who had remained silent for the whole discussion (and looking rather angry), suddenly burst out, "But don't you see, everything is extraordinary, everything is a miracle. Why are you just singling out particular experiences as being more special than others? What could be more extraordinary than all of us living on a little ball spinning around in space! We live in the middle of one, huge miracle".

Unlike the evening with the potato chips, this gathering quickly recovered momentum after George's emotional eruption and proceeded as smoothly as I had hoped. But looking back after many years, I realise now that his words changed me fundamentally. They went so deep at the time that I didn't realise their effect, but they expressed the fundamental spiritual question – "What is this?" It is when this question, however expressed, enters the warp and weave of our consciousness that everything changes. A growing awareness of the utter mysteriousness of this moment begins to be the backdrop for everything. Our very experience of life is slowly transformed.

Over the years, I have often pondered the paradox that George presented. Consciously, he struggled badly to find meaning and cope with the practicalities of living. Despite being a really nice bloke, he could be insensitive with regard to the impact of his words and actions on those around. He often lived unwisely, causing himself physical and psychological damage. Yet there could be moments when, seemingly without his realising, he could express astonishingly deep spiritual insight or through some action lead another to a new place. The everyday George was simply not capable of these moments.

It has become clear to me that there was a "presence" or "loving intelligence" that, from time to time, expressed itself through George. My encounters with George were, I now see, a clear demonstration that we do not walk the spiritual path alone. Guidance and inspiration are present for those who have ears to hear. Perhaps we call this "voice" the Holy Spirit, or the Buddha Wisdom, or the Arwen, or by another of the many names by which it is known. My experience with George, because of the contrast with his everyday self, has clearly shown me that there is a wonderful reality behind these words.

This leads me to a challenging thought. What if this voice is talking to us all the time through others, trying to make itself heard? What if I only heard it through George because of its stark contrast with my image of who he was? Perhaps if only we were to listen with a truly silent mind to whoever is in front of us, we would start to hear marvellous things. Of course, another word for such listening is "contemplation" – the art of paying profound attention to what is. This is why contemplation is prayer

The voice of wisdom must also be present in you and me, teaching and guiding in its own enigmatic way. Perhaps another teaching that George offers is that I must not become disabled by guilt when my thoughts, words and actions are not wise or loving. Perhaps he can help me to remember that beneath the chaos, that marvellous presence awaits its moment. He can help me not to take the dramas of my personality too seriously.

And could it be that the Voice, the Sacred Presence that rests beneath the surface of life, is the greater part of who George, you and I truly are?

Thank you George.

Contemplation and Problems

I think it was Einstein who said, "the consciousness that creates a problem can never solve it".

As I have observed my mind, I have increasingly seen this to be true.

The words have become a bridge, linking the practice of contemplation with the challenge of living in the everyday world.

Too often, I have identified something in my life as a problem and my mind has tied itself in knots trying to find a solution. There may be too many possible answers and I don't know which to choose, or perhaps there seems to be no way forward. In either case, the experience has been one of turmoil and worry, often impacting on those around.

Sometimes, not often enough, I have remembered Einstein's words and have sought instead a deeper consciousness. As my mind has stilled and become less noisy, on many occasions the way forward has become obvious. At other times something even more interesting has happened – I have seen that no problem really exists. The "problem" is actually just an illusion created by a confused mind, existing in a dream-like state.

For a long time now I have acted as a spiritual companion to all kinds of people. Many come to me because there is a situation in their life that is problematic. They hope that by talking to me the answer will become apparent. I have learned that my role is not to enter into the perceived problem, but to nurture a shift of consciousness, in both of us, to a deeper and more still place. I have become sensitive as to when this occurs and have seen again and again that it is in this quality of mind that either the way forward becomes apparent (which frequently involves doing nothing) or the problem disappears.

In the stillness, I have often also become aware of a wisdom present that is more than the two of us.

The stillness has become the prayer of listening. In the quiet a "voice", which previously was drowned out, makes itself known (usually in a way beyond words). And the voice speaks from a place where our life (and its problems) is seen in an infinitely greater context.

It is not uncommon for me to say very little during a session, yet often the person leaves looking as though they have put down a great weight.

It is also not uncommon for them to reappear a month or two later, once more lost in turmoil. Life has taken them out of inner stillness and that deep connection, back into confusion. This is why the spiritual path is a practice - a way of life. Deep habits of thinking, constantly reinforced by the society in which we live, cannot be changed overnight.

Spirituality is not a magic pill.

Interestingly, even though I am aware of the truth of this insight, I still find myself on occasion tearing at a problem like a dog with a bone. Something in me refuses to stop, enter stillness and see the situation in a new way. There seems to be something in me that wants to have a problem, which seeks victim-hood. It will present convincing arguments to justify feeling as I do. Yet to justify needless suffering is madness. On such occasions it can require real determination to see differently, but the relief is enormous when I finally do so.

For me, therefore, the spiritual path (of which the practice of contemplation is a fundamental strand) is not essentially about problem solving. It is concerned with changing the quality of consciousness so that we may view the world from a deeper place of clarity. In this place we make ourselves available to encounter that to which the word "God" points.

And also in this place, as a by-product, insight will frequently arise regarding the passing, temporary challenges of our worldly life.

The Impossibility of Peaceful Agitation

Most people do not want peace.

They think they do, but deceive themselves.

They really want peaceful agitation or, if you prefer, agitated peacefulness. They want a life of surface stimulation, shallow variety, exciting frenzy and righteous conflict.

And they want to be peaceful.

They are dismayed and puzzled when peace proves elusive. Something must be wrong, they say. Someone must be to blame. It's the world's fault they are not peaceful.

Nevertheless, occasionally, all will taste peace as a natural experience, but it may not be recognised. It may not match their idea of peace. Instead, it may be perceived as a boring wilderness, desolate, empty and barren. There is no agitation to stir the mind.

Yet it is in the wilderness that peace is found. But someone must be willing to stay there for as long as is needed.

Eventually, if they are brave enough, the desert will become a fathomless ocean, into which they may sink and discover deeper realities.

If they are brave enough. If they are willing to open to peace itself.

If they are willing to let go, completely, of their need for agitation.

Where We Stand

I think from where we stand the rain seems random. If we could stand somewhere else, we would see the order in it.
(TONY HILLERMAN; "COYOTE WAITS")

Approaching God is like climbing a mountain.

Perhaps we start our journey on a bright sunny morning. From our base camp we gaze at the view. We note the heights of the different mountains, the patches of snow, the small streams running down the sides and the green of the valleys. It is very easy to believe we are seeing everything as it is.

We start to climb and eventually tiredness arises, so we establish another camp. While sitting there we look around again. Now our view is changed and things are not the same.

What we see depends where we are on the mountain. There is no complete view; no total understanding. This is only a problem if we make it so.

Shifting truth is disturbing. It is natural to yearn for certainty. It is tempting to stay where we are, or even to go back down the mountain. But if we want to reach the summit, we must keep climbing.

Know, though, that nothing can prepare us for the summit. For on the summit, as we stare into the clear sky, there is nothing but infinity and formlessness.

A Warning

We should not seek inner peace if it is not what we really want.
  Otherwise we will experience great confusion. We will encounter inner turmoil, not inner peace.
  We must be devastatingly honest with ourselves. If we really want an exciting and interesting life in the world, we must admit that this is so. We also need to accept that this will not be a peaceful life; it will offer different fruits.
  We must find out what we really want and then be true to ourselves.
  The few who truly seek inner peace will discover a path that is, at times, difficult. It will require courage and determination. Only those whose hearts are true to this path will reach journey's end.
  Be warned, though, journey's end is not of this world.

The Poetry of Truth

Truth is the ultimate simplicity.
Truth is simply the way things are.
God is truth.
Truth can never be grasped by thought, because truth is always whole and complete, whereas thought is no more than a collection of fragments; shards of a broken mirror that arise after truth has passed.
We observe the universe and see consistency, cause and effect, and predictable consequences. We call these "laws". So we have the laws of gravitation, of light, of energy and so forth. In our minds we conceive of these laws as existing in a tangible way, yet we know that the law of gravity will never be isolated in a test-tube. Such laws are not a part of the universe; they simply manifest within it and energy dances to the music they play.
Such laws are of God and emanate from beyond energy.
But laws are not the truth. They are merely, in their own way, descriptions of the truth. Laws that describe cause and effect, sequences, consequences and mechanisms only have existence within time.
Truth exists outside time.
Truth only ever exists at a causal level; it is never an effect.
The cause of everything we experience lies outside

time. Thought can only exist within time and can never comprehend truth. The premise of all logic exists outside time and can therefore never be realised within thought.

Truth exists in timelessness.

Religion is the search for truth. It is therefore the search for encounter. It is not the search for intellectual constructs or verbal formulations. Religion is about becoming vulnerable to the reality of what is, not a description of what is. It involves immersion and integration with existence; not separation and abstraction, which is the nature of thought. Immersion is baptism.

To open to truth requires a journey; a pilgrimage. There is no magic pill that produces instant results. This is a pilgrimage of unlearning, letting go of the layers of thought that lie between truth and us.

The role of thought in religion is to produce unlearning. The only purpose of thought is to negate other thought. It is a meeting of thought that results in no thought.

Truth is the ultimate simplicity.

One could imagine that truth is the equivalent of zero and we are lost in a fragmented world of positive and negative numbers. Numbers are simply a description of fragmentation. No number can ever be whole. Only zero is complete. In this picture, one could visualise the search for truth as the coming together of a negative and positive of the same value. Their meeting results in the death of both, but also in the revelation of the transcendent zero; an experience of wholeness and completion.

Thought is a broken mind; a mind in pieces, desperately trying to re-assemble itself. Always in the past, never in the present. A mind fragmented into a million shining diamonds; like a shattered mirror or crystal.

For this process of healing to occur, for the experience of truth to be revealed, beliefs and doctrines must be seen as doorways to what lies beyond. These doorways are to be found between ideas. The doorframe is formed by our beliefs, thoughts and ideas, but they are not in themselves the opening. When two conflicting ideas are held together in the mind, in peace and without choice, a gateway is revealed. With the exercise of patience and choice-less awareness both, in time, will die and something infinitely greater will be born.

This is how thought must be used in the search for the experience of truth.

But such a process can only arise within order. Also, ideas have to be grasped with commitment, before they can be transcended. Religious traditions of true depth offer "holy order" so that this process may occur. Commitment to a tradition in humility is a wonderful path. The integrity of the beliefs and doctrines of that tradition must be firmly respected and completely valued in order that the road through them may be cleared.

Gratitude of the deepest kind is the only true response to a tradition that makes such a gift. It is offering to live in us so that it may die, to allow something greater to be born.

Truth is born and dies in every moment.

Beauty and truth are two words for the same experience. The beauty of a sunset is only experienced in the moment before thought engages. When truth is remembered, it is no longer true. All thought is memory. A total experience of a moment will never involve memory.

The world of thought is like a narcotic drug to which we are addicted. We have been addicted for so long that we mistake the haze, the distortion, the drunken stupor, for reality.

Prayer

Prayer is very simple.

We learn about prayer by doing it.

Prayer is a living relationship with God. It involves all those simple normal activities that constitute a relationship with a human being. It involves eye contact, body language, talking, listening, sharing experiences. It involves love, joy, anger, sadness.

It is profound intimacy.

It requires commitment for better and for worse, for richer or poorer, in sickness and in health. It calls for patience, trust and faith.

The relationship of prayer exists waking and sleeping, for the whole of every day, for all of our lives. We can relate to God at any time, in any place. Only our misconceived belief that prayer is a special activity leads us to believe that particular times and places must be set aside.

It would be a strange marriage where the husband and wife talked only on a Sunday morning at 10.30 am; and only then by way of rituals and words composed by other people.

Real prayer is like marriage. Jesus frequently used this image in his teaching. It is a continuing, constant experience of communication in all its varied forms; communication so intimate, on occasion, that it becomes communion.

Chess Lessons

Entries in a spiritual journal are rarely the last word on the topic they are discussing.

By their very nature they are addressing deep matters of the soul, which often frustratingly defy clear expression in words.

But the very effort of trying can sometimes bring a degree of clarity. Attempting to say out-loud, whether to a journal or to another person who is really listening, what is whirling around inside often produces insight.

And in this process nothing is sacred except the practice of devastating honesty. Consistency does not matter, only truth.

The following words should be seen in this light. They reflect a work in progress.

I recently played in a chess tournament. I had not played for many years. It was a bit of a shock in a number of ways.

It is one of the world's best-kept secrets that once upon a time I was a pretty good player, to the extent that for a while I devoted myself to chess on a full-time basis. Eventually, however, I drifted away from the game. I realised that I actually didn't enjoy chess itself, but the very temporary thrill of winning – which is a sure-fire recipe for suffering.

Recently the thought came to mind of making a comeback. I am sure that a strand of this impulse was the fact that it is very difficult to give up something that you are good at. In chess I was "somebody".

I also wondered if, after many years of spiritual enquiry and practice, I would be able to play the game in a different way. Perhaps I would be able to concentrate on the creative side of the game (like mathematics, chess is capable of great beauty) rather than the competitive.

So I entered a tournament being held near to where I live.

Things did not go well.

In fact, I had my worst ever result in a tournament of this type. Even when starting out as a teenager, I never scored so poorly. It was a chastening experience. More than that, I still did not enjoy the game itself. I told my wife that entering the tournament had resolved the question in my mind – I would not be playing again.

Then something strange happened. Over the next few days I found myself drawn once more to the idea of playing, despite what had happened. I began to rationalize about how if I just did a bit of work, I could get back to my previous standard; how I could then play creatively rather than competitively; and how it must be right to express a talent.

All those years of spiritual enquiry and practice have, however, taught me to be suspicious of such rationalizations. The mind has many veils. So I have been trying to look deeper to see where this impulse is coming from.

Part of it is, I am sure, hurt pride. My self-image has been severely dented. Even though I have not been playing, my standing as "a good chess player" has been an important element in my sense of identity. I want it back.

But I have begun to see that something deeper is also at work; my need for clear structure, objectives and, most importantly, outcomes. This is a need that I didn't realise I had.

I have begun to see that for years I may have been struggling with the ill-defined nature of the spiritual life. The results (especially the benefits) of all the practice, effort, soul-searching and life-changing decisions can be difficult to see.

Indeed, it may not be at all clear what positive results might look like.

When outcomes are not clear, it can be difficult sometimes to find the energy and motivation to keep going.

It is so often only in looking back that any objective measure of progress can been seen. Or perhaps from an unexpected comment by an old acquaintance about how much more peaceful we now are, or how well we now listen.

But perhaps deep down I want more than this; I want to clearly see what is happening and be able to respond accordingly. I suppose I want to be in control.

The truth, however, is that walking the spiritual path is an act of faith, in response to a deep inner impulse that cannot be denied. And it may well be that the impulse is not even mine, but is a response to a call from a level of reality immeasurably deeper than "me".

Viewed this way, the desire to be in control looks a bit silly.

For much of the time we must be content with a subjective, rather than objective, sense of progress. We have to keep walking the path, content with an intuitive sense that we are going in the right direction, rather than seeking to mark off stages of the journey on some kind of spiritual map.

I wonder also whether I have been struggling with the spiritual focus on the "now". Perhaps part of my mind wants a plan, full of aims and objectives, to which to give itself. Being "in the present" is all well and good, but without a plan for the future the reservoir of creative energy within each of us can begin to stagnate

My experience with the chess tournament suggests, much to my surprise, that I may have been struggling with all of this. It has left a suspicion that my desire to return to chess playing is, in part, a rebellion against the unplanned, amorphous, faith-demanding mysteriousness of the spiritual life.

Perhaps chess has become a symbol for my mind of this

sense of discomfort.

The chess board is a small, closed world of systematic rules and consequences. It has objective structure and outcomes. What has occurred can be clearly seen and firm plans for improvement laid for the future. It provides its own focus and way forward.

I may not enjoy chess, but at least I know what is happening and where I should be aiming. It is very tempting to live once more in such a small, predictable world rather than in the limitless universe of deep contemplative mystery.

Of course, I could always try to reduce the Mystery to the spiritual equivalent of chess. I could embrace a religious belief system of absolute truths, ethics and authority (probably based on a book) with a clear reward system of predictable consequences for good and bad behaviour, and a non-negotiable vision of the future.

Tempting as this sounds, however, it would not work. I cannot live a lie. Chess in its own terms is true – it is a small, closed system of immutable laws. But I know that the awesome ineffability of existence cannot be reduced to this, easier though it may seem to make life.

So I must keep faithfully walking into the dazzling darkness, trusting my inner compass, knowing that for reasons I can never really understand I can do no other.

But I must also keep questioning everything that happens.

The Shocking Ordinariness of Death

Contemplation is often called the way of unknowing, for it reveals the hollowness of the stories we tell ourselves about life.

This is not an intellectual process, but a practice of clear seeing. When the mind is still and the vortex of stories we are constantly telling ourselves has diminished, when the distorting veils of belief have become transparent, all that remains is reality itself.

But do we want reality? Our stories bring comfort and a sense of meaning. Is the truth too much?

A while ago I watched a television programme about an American army field hospital during the Iraq conflict. It was a powerful experience.

Its power arose from the way it was made. The camera simply observed. It was a silent watcher in the room. It moved as little as possible. Any narration was minimal, just sufficient to ensure that the viewer understood what was happening. No story was imposed. There was no music or other sound effects

The camera became a metaphor for contemplation. It encouraged contemplation in the viewer.

A young, nameless soldier was rushed into the hospital in critical condition. Shrapnel from a roadside bomb had damaged his heart.

The camera watched as the doctors set to work.

Emergency surgery was performed and, for a while, the staff were optimistic that he would recover. But a few hours after the operation, without regaining consciousness, he began to slip away. The faces of the doctors and nurses, and their body language, spoke volumes. They obviously knew that there was little hope, but they gathered themselves and tried again anyway.

Then his heart stopped beating.

Defibrillation and massage had no effect.

Eventually, with a few quiet words, the senior doctor declared the young man to be dead. He was gone.

The medical staff stepped back and the time of death was recorded.

The camera watched the staff as they adjusted to what had happened. There was no outward display of emotion, but they seemed to shrink into themselves. Nothing was said. Each was lost in thought as they cleaned-up the room. The observer was left with an impression of profound disturbance, but below the surface.

The body was placed in a black, zip-up body bag. The camera continued to watch as it was wheeled to the mortuary, a stark, stone-built storage facility, and placed in a row of other bodies. The camera lingered on the neatly arranged black bags for a short while. Nothing was said.

I was shaken to the core.

It took a while to understand what I was feeling. It was easy to miss, because my mind did not want to acknowledge what it had realised. It was desperate to cling to its stories.

The sense of deep, primal shock arose from the insight that nothing fundamental had happened.

My mind screamed out that a human being had died. A young man , with his life ahead of him, full of hopes and dreams, loved and loving, was no more. It felt like the universe should pause in horror and bow its head.

Yet the universe did not stop. It just carried on, as though he had never been.

The ordinariness of what I had witnessed had shattered something in my mind.

I saw that for thousands of years, where the Tigris and Euphrates rivers meet, young men have killed each other. Countless lives have been taken in just that one small place on the Earth's surface. Their names are lost; most forgotten within a few years of their deaths. This time it was a young man from America, but he too will soon be forgotten. Those who loved him will suffer terrible anguish, but the truth is that they too will soon be dead.

I saw that everything dies. Planets die; suns die; galaxies die; even the universe itself will end.

The narrative that had been instilled into me, from childhood, around the specialness of death had been revealed for what it was; simply a story.

In the vastness of time and space our lives are seemingly insignificant. We do not want to acknowledge this obvious truth.

This shattering insight was not the fruit of thinking. It flowered in a still mind, in an instant, as if from nowhere. The truth does not require thought, for it is the way things are. Only seeing is required.

The fruits of contemplation can seem bitter indeed. But only the truth can set us free.

And some time after the shattering came a sense of liberation. It is an experience of liberation that defies language and ideas. The best that I can do is what follows.

Each of us is a part of something extraordinary, but we don't see it. We are too close, so see very little, and what we do see is unfocussed and distorted.

Imagine a most wonderful jigsaw puzzle. A single piece may be full of colour and intriguing shapes, but has no meaning on its own. Only by stepping back and seeing the whole picture does the single piece reveal its truth.

If we expand our focus away from the human body and personality, which so entrance us, there is something else to be seen.

If we step back and pay attention to the unfolding of existence itself, of which our lives are but an expression, a sense of awe and mystery arises.

To see the constant flow of birth and death, arising and ceasing, allows a profound wonder to surface.

That young soldier's life was special, but not in the way we usually think. The very fact of his birth was extraordinary; and the fact of his death equally so. Existence itself is inexpressible, awe-inspiring and humbling. So therefore must be that which exists within existence.

As I then contemplated the death of the young soldier, compassion and sadness arose. But these feeling were now held in a vast, majestic space, within the great all-encompassing mystery. They are no longer everything, but jewels of light against a mighty backdrop.

They are known from love, not fear.

Parable of Dave

I used to work with Dave.

He was very clever and rapidly making his way up the career ladder. But, like many clever people, he was a bit eccentric. We were accustomed to odd things happening around him.

One day Dave was late arriving for work. This was alarming as he had an important meeting that morning. Much to our relief, he eventually burst into the office and collapsed into a chair. He was a mess. The nice suit he had put on for the meeting was creased and covered in mud. There was even a tear in one of the trouser legs. His hair was a complete tangle and the remains of a small, unidentifiable flower protruded from his collar.

"Dave, what happened", we cried, knowing we were in for a good tale.

"Well", he said drawing a deep breath, "Something rather strange happened to me on the way to work".

He then told the following dramatic story.

Earlier that morning, resplendent in his best suit, Dave had made ready to leave home for the office. He had strapped his briefcase onto the back of his moped and then inspected the weather. The sky was clear and blue, with a bright sun. Obviously no need for a coat, he had concluded, and had simply wrapped a thick woolly scarf around his neck, tucking it in firmly below his helmet. He had then set off, the small engine on his moped chugging away.

Dave lived out in the country and had to wind his way along narrow, muddy lanes to reach the main road. At first all was well, but then the problems started.

A thick fog had descended.

This had surprised him because it had been so clear only a short time before. He had slowed down and concentrated as hard as he could. Yet, despite his best efforts, he had started to weave about, finding it difficult to keep to the correct side of the road. The visibility was too bad.

Then, hurtling out of the fog had come a car, displaying no lights, only just missing him. The driver had glared at Dave as though he was an idiot. This had made Dave furious, both at the crazy driving in such thick fog and at the injustice. No wonder there were so many accidents in fog, he had raged.

He also had difficulty avoiding the potholes that littered the narrow lanes. These could be lethal for those on two wheels. His anger had then shifted to the local council for failing to do their duty.

By the time he reached the main road he was in a foul mood. He was also rather worried about continuing the journey; but the meeting was important so he ploughed on.

Joining the stream of traffic on the main road had been a nightmare. The fog had become even thicker and a steady stream of traffic had been hurtling along without any apparent sense of danger. Dave had heard of multiple crashes caused by fog and could now understand how they happened. He had been shocked by the stupidity of so many people, risking not just their own lives but others as well.

Eventually, he had dived into a gap in the traffic and ridden slowly and carefully along. His safety-first approach had not gone down well with many of the other drivers and he had been subjected to shaking fists and blaring horns. The lorries had been the worst. Monstrous, roaring beasts that had tailgated his little moped before surging past with little room to spare.

By this point he had been both furious and scared.

And then, almost inevitably, disaster had occurred.

One moment he had been slowly riding along, trying to make out the road through the haze. The next he was flying through the air, still on his bike, having hit a kerbstone head-on. A few moments later the moped had crash-landed onto some muddy grass, ploughing through a mixture of soil and plants. It had then hit a tree, causing him to fly over the handle bars, landing with a thud in a nice flower bed.

Dave had been pretty shaken-up. He had gingerly got to his feet, relieved to discover that apart from a few minor aches he seemed uninjured.

He had then removed his helmet.

A simple act, but a moment of revelation.

The fog disappeared. The sunshine and the blue sky were back.

With a sigh he had then realised the truth. He pulled out a handkerchief and wiped the condensation from inside the visor. Then he loosened the scarf, which he had tucked-in too well, thereby blocking the flow of air within the helmet.

He had stood there for short while in the middle of the traffic island. He had noticed the black mark where his tyre had struck the kerb, the muddy furrow across the grass and the carnage he had wrought in the once lovely municipal flowerbed. It was a small blessing that the ornamental tree that had brought his progress to such a sudden halt did not seem damaged.

He had tried not to notice the bemused looks of passing drivers, as they stared at the battered figure standing in the middle of the traffic island.

Fortunately, he had been able to restart the moped and finish his journey.

~

This a good story. Once we know that Dave is alright it

brings a smile to the face. Dave was laughing as he recounted his adventure.

But this is not why I tell it.

I share the story as a parable of the relationship that most of us have with our minds, most of the time.

I invite you to ponder what I mean by this. A parable explained loses its power.

~

I have sometimes used this parable when leading a retreat. To end the session, I ask the question, "What was Dave's problem?"

On every occasion the instant answer has come back, "It's obvious, he couldn't see".

Actually, this is not correct. Dave's problem was that he did not know that he could not see.

If he had realised the visor was misted over, he would have cleaned it. No decision would have been needed. The necessary action was self-evident.

This is an important aspect of the parable that may reveal much about our own lives.

The Pond

The pond is still and clear. Not a ripple disturbs its surface.
    We stand at the edge, entranced by the peace.
    Yet we cannot resist the urge. We have to do it. We reach down, pick up a stone and throw it into the pond. Instantly, the stillness is gone. We are dismayed, yet pick up more stones and fling those in also. Ripples spread everywhere, becoming waves that clash with each other, creating more chaos.
    The wondrous stillness and clarity has gone. Something precious has been lost, but we are the cause. We seem to be at war with ourselves. We want things that cannot survive together. We claim to want one thing, but do another.
    What are we to do?
    We must stop throwing stones. And we must investigate why we want to throw stones.
    Nothing else must matter.

The Humming Bird

The humming bird is a remarkable creature.

It is the only bird that can fly backwards, as well as forwards. It can also hover, fly straight up and down, sideways and on its back.

But it is impossible for the human eye to see how it achieves such feats.

Its wings flap seventy times per second. They are a blur to the observer. The bird's very name is a description of the sound the wings make at such speed.

Only the miracle of modern video technology allows us to see, and thereby understand, how a humming bird does such things. By slowing down images of the bird in flight, it becomes possible to see how its wings work.

The human mind is an infinitely more remarkable creation. It puts the humming bird to shame

It tries to fly in many different directions in the same moment, at the speed of light. It creates its own hum, which too often resembles more of a cacophony. For most of us this is its default state, most of the time.

Individually and collectively we see nothing with clarity, create a false reality out of what we believe we see and then live in chaos. Confusion and suffering become our experience, so deeply rooted that we confuse them with normality.

The speed, fragmentation and confusion of our thinking makes it impossible to understand what is happening to our minds. Healing seems impossible, so we settle for the suffering. It is the devil we know.

But we can understand what is happening if, as with the humming bird's wings, we find a way to slow everything down.

Understanding leads to transcendence.

Contemplation is the spiritual equivalent of the camera. Through focussing the energy of the fragmented mind a coherence arises, the hurricane of thought slows down and clarity emerges. It is a peace that, once tasted, is never forgotten. It is the peace of the present moment.

And this can become prayer, for the depths of now is the only place where God may be encountered.

The Possibility of Change

There is something inspiring when two great spiritual teachers, from different traditions and epochs, give the same message.

I once saw a television programme about a western woman who for many years had been a Tibetan Buddhist nun. This had included a long period living as a solitary hermit in a Himalayan cave.

The part of the programme that really grabbed my attention, and has stayed with me ever since, was a talk she gave later in life to a room full of Nepalese farmers. It contained none of the sublime, penetrating philosophy that we usually associate with Buddhism. Instead, the nun kept repeating in different ways the same simple message – "we can change".

At first, I was taken aback by the simplicity of her teaching. It seemed too obvious. Barely worth saying. After a while, however, I began to see what an important idea this was. It slowly dawned that if this claim were not true, the spiritual path goes nowhere. It is a great illusion.

Also, as I contemplated this teaching, I began to see how easy it would be to believe that change was impossible. That I am what I am, and could never be any different.

I thought about all those times when I had tried to change some habitual behaviour and remembered how hard it was. St Paul's words from chapter seven of Romans came to mind – "I do not understand my own actions. For I do not do what I want, but do the very thing that I hate".

As we grow up, we become a complex of conditioned responses to the world. We are made from the outside inwards. Many of these habitual patterns are beneficial and enable us to function better in life. But some, as we all know too well, hurt ourselves and those around. Yet despite seeing the damage we are doing, we seem unable to stop. So perhaps we justify our actions with clever rationalisation, or blame others for making us act in this way. For some, the impact of terrible experiences, particularly in childhood, has laid down such deep traits that this teaching can provoke anger, as it can appear to devalue the trauma that has been suffered. And, more than anything else, this pattern of programmed responses becomes who we think we are. It becomes our identity.

But somewhere, deep down, our reasons do not fool us and crippling feelings of guilt grow remorselessly.

The words of the wise nun came back last Sunday as I sat in a church and listened to the story of John the Baptist. Wrapped up in the traditional language of the Bible, product of an ancient and alien culture, yet the same teaching – "you can change". Using the powerful symbol of baptism in water to wash away the past (and expressing himself far more forcefully than the gentle nun!) he sought to help people free themselves from the habits of the mind that cause so much suffering – and to release the terrible, subterranean guilt that went with this. He brought hope that the future could be better than the past, if we really wanted.

Yet do we really want to change?

It's easy to say the words, but meaning them is something else entirely. To change, to let go of powerful habitual thought patterns, is a form of death. We are very attached to the devil we know. Also, as St Paul discovered, to truly change can be very difficult.

I think that John's response to this would have been simple. It would have reflected the fact that he was not a philosopher or a psychologist, but a spiritual teacher.

He would have said that we are never alone. That there is always a presence with us, which he would have called the Holy Spirit, waiting to help. He would have said that by truly becoming willing to change, we create a virtuous circle in which that presence can enter into our depths, to slowly unravel that which causes so much suffering. This in turn inspires us to grapple with yet more change. It is our committed willingness that matters – willingness as prayer.

I think he would have said something else as well.

He would have said that such clearing of the mind is the beginning of the journey, not the end. That in the spaciousness and peace that is created, that spiritual presence can grow and flourish into something transcendent; something holy.

Which is the point where John fades from the picture and the Mystery of Jesus enters.

Invisible Journey

It is very easy to feel that we are making no progress on the contemplative path. Indeed, it is easy to think sometimes that we are going backwards.

This is because it is a path of unknowing, of unlearning what we thought we knew.

Our false certainties, which brought so much comfort, will drop away. Things that brought us pleasure in life may lose their taste, as we no longer seek their anaesthesia. Relationships may begin to drift apart as we change.

There will come a point, however, when looking back we will see that enormous progress has occurred. We will struggle to recognise the person we used to be. More than anything, our sense of the great mystery of existence will have grown.

Yet we will struggle to identify when the shifts in consciousness happened. Looking back can give us faith to continue.

Wind Chimes

Wind chimes do nothing.
    They remain perfectly still, until the wind blows. Then they make beautiful sound.
    When the wind stops, they become perfectly still once more.
    Chimes do not cling to the beautiful sound they made.
    The wind will blow again and they will make more beautiful sound, but always different to last time. It will be ever new.
    Wind chimes are always at peace.
    Effortless peace.
    Effortless creation.

From the Gospel of Thomas:

> *Jesus said, "If they ask you,*
> *'What is the sign of your father within you?'*
> *say to them, 'It is movement, and rest.'"*

Bliss

Bliss is a quiet experience. Joy is a quiet experience.

These are two words for the same experience; an upwelling of pure being from the depths of who we are.

We cannot generate bliss, but we can remove the mind-blocks that dam its flow.

I have noticed that bliss arises when something new is born in my mind; in that moment when I grow in awareness.

In such moments the world seems to quietly shine.

I have also noticed that I must not cling to the moment, to the new insight, to the joy of bliss, but must let it pass on its way. It's nature is always to flow. It will return in a new form in its own time.

To cling to bliss is to kill it. To live, bliss must be always new.

Some words from Meister Eckhart:

Every action of God is new, for he makes all things new.
God is the newest thing there is; the youngest thing there is.
God is the beginning and if we become united to him
we become new again.

Magic and Love

Fourteen years ago my wife and I had a magical experience.

We had just finished a conversation over lunch as to whether to have another cat. We had lost one a few months before on a nearby busy road. We were both certain that we would not be doing so.

As we started to take our plates through to the kitchen, my wife heard a scraping sound on the back door. She went to see what it was and called me over. Through the glass we could see two little legs pumping away, trying to get attention. We opened the door and in walked a young, brown tabby cat, who went straight up the stairs and curled-up on our youngest son's bed.

It was one of those moments when the astonishing synchronicity of an event takes your breath away.

Megan, as she became known, stayed with us for fourteen years and quietly became part of the fabric of our family. She was the most intelligent cat I have ever encountered and possessed a highly developed personality.

Megan died a few days ago after a period of illness. I cannot remember the last time I felt so sad. Megan has taught me how to cry again. I was not expecting this. I knew that I would be sorrowful when she died, but was totally unprepared for the power of my grief.

It may well be that I will never fully understand why I

have been so affected. At the moment all I have are fragments.

One fragment is the realisation that from Megan I have experienced a beautifully pure love. In the days leading up to her death, she could not move very much and required careful nursing. In order to speak to her I had to get down onto the floor and look into her eyes. Shining back at me was a love that was unconditional and total.

Also shining back at me was life in all its mystery. An alien mind that I could never hope to really understand, yet also the same life force that is in me, meeting itself in her.

Another fragment is the existential shock of her "goneness". One moment she was there, and the next she was gone. The totality of the ending is something I find difficult to take in. Time has moved on and will not return.

But then something happened that enveloped my grief within something wondrous and enigmatic.

Megan's life with us started in magic and ended in magic.

A day after she died, I got angry with God and railed that someone so beautiful could be no more, to be eventually forgotten. I asked with all my heart that I would be given a sign that she was alright – that she still lived in some way.

An hour or so later I received an email from our youngest son (who's bed Megan had gone straight to when she first arrived). He had not been sure whether to mention something, but thought that he had better. He has a rather sceptical mind.

The previous evening, before he had known of Megan's death, he had been walking home and had suddenly heard a loud "meow". He had looked around immediately, but could not see any cat. He turned to walk away and heard the same sound again. Once more there was nothing to be seen.

Perhaps my prayer was answered before it was expressed.

Emergence

When I was training to be a priest we were taken to visit a funeral director.

In one of the viewing rooms was a body in an open coffin. One of my younger colleagues had never seen a dead body before and was moved by the experience. Afterwards he tried to articulate his feelings, but had great difficulty. All he could manage was something along the lines of, "the thing about dead bodies is, well, they are very, very dead aren't they".

Even though he seemed to be stating the obvious, we all knew what he meant. Something indefinable was missing. The form was still human, but "not real". It was like looking at a waxwork or a life-size doll. It wasn't like someone who was asleep, who happened not be breathing.

Even now, I struggle to express what we all felt. But there will be many reading these words who will also understand what he meant.

This experience came to mind recently as I read a book by a famous scientist. He wrote about how difficult it is, scientifically, to define both what life is and when it is absent. No formula or set of words seems to be sufficient to pin it down. Biology, chemistry and physics all have their own definitions.

Yet, as the scientist noted, we all know when life is

present and when it is gone. We do not know how we know, but we do.

All he felt able to say about life was that it was an emergent phenomenon. When conditions were right in the material world, it seemed to manifest from a deeper place within the fabric of existence. From our level of reality, we could recognise its presence but not understand what it was.

The implications of this statement are awesome. It is a reminder that we have no idea what or who we are; that the soap opera of our daily lives is lived out in the midst of utter mystery.

It humbles us by pointing out that if we do not even know the most fundamental thing about our existence, all the rest of our presumed knowledge must be treated with caution.

To contemplate these truths for even a few moments cannot but blow our minds wide open.

But the scientist did not stop there.

He suggested that alongside emergent life was emergent knowing, which he called intuition, very different to the kind of thought-based rational knowing with which we are so familiar.

For him this would be the explanation for how my friends and I reacted to the body in the funeral parlour. We knew that something was no longer present, but could not begin to say what it was.

Of course, mystical spirituality has been saying this for centuries.

That this world is an effect, emanating from a causal realm enfolded within and around what we experience as everyday reality.

That incarnate in this world as corporeal beings, we too are an effect of a much deeper causal self, who's knowing can emerge into our embodied minds when appropriate.

That as we open to this relationship through the practice of stillness and surrender, this stream can become a river.

In the western tradition, this expression of knowing was once called gnosis, although this is a much abused term.

Very interestingly, the scientist identified one more possible emergent phenomenon. That at the heart of all emergence there may be a purpose and intent that lies behind everything. We might use the word God (another much abused word) to describe this fundamental presence. But because it is emergent, it could never be known by thought-based consciousness. Only through what he called "intuition" could it enter awareness. Such emergent knowing had nothing to do with belief and certainty, but naturally finds its home in a profound, active agnosticism.

As with the boundary between life and death, it is difficult to see any difference between this approach and the way of apophatic theology, within which contemplation finds its home.

It is the way of mystery. The way that demands we acknowledge what we don't know, before trying to work out what we do.

The first part of the process is for most of us an endeavour that lasts a lifetime.

Joy

Joy is letting go, which is freedom.
    The ties that bind us are of our own making. Every time we want something, we bind ourselves a little more. Every time that we withhold, we are held. Every time that we seek to acquire, we give away our power.
    Joy rests in valuing nothing and everything. Joy excludes comparison and weighing. To joy, everything is the same. Thus, to pass from one moment to another does not involve a stepping down or a stepping up. Joy is therefore permanent.
    Joy is not of time. It does not exist in the past or in the future. It can only be experienced now. We all too readily scan our memories for times when we think that we felt joy, and seek to relive what is no more. In this lies suffering. We look to the future to create situations which we think will bring us joy, but this too is suffering.
    Joy is now. Desire and wanting are not now; they are past and future.
    Permanent joy is an acknowledgement of impermanence. It is an acceptance of the way things are.
    To be joyful is to be light. It is to put aside forever the burdens of the past and the future which weigh us down.
    It is to be constant.

A Baby's Eyes

Jesus said, "A person of great age will not hesitate to ask a little child seven days old about the place of Life, and he will live, for all those who are first will become last, and they will become a single one".

(GOSPEL OF THOMAS)

I once got lost in a baby's eyes.

It was unexpected, in stark contrast to the challenging situation I was in at the time.

The baby was placed into my arms and, as I glanced down at its face, I became transfixed. Two fathomless pools of pure life caught me and the harsh world faded into the background.

Communion occurred. Something in the depths of my soul recognised itself in the child's shining eyes. There was no gap. What shone out of the baby's eyes also shone out of mine.

The virginal awareness of the child was all that it knew. Yet that would quickly change as it grew older. Very soon it would acquire a personality, a history, anxieties, desires and opinions. That vast sea of pure awareness would shrink and freeze into a tiny fearful person in this fleeting world, as it had with me.

But not forever, Jesus tells us, if we are willing to lift our heads from the intense story in which we have become lost.

We must step back and find our true self; that mysterious light that shines out of a baby's eyes.

The light asks us who we want to be.

It is the deathless light of God, at the heart of all that is. It is our eternal, undying self. It is inconceivably more.

After a while the difficult world came back into awareness, but I was changed forever.

More from the Gospel of Thomas.

The disciples said to Jesus, "Speak to us about our end: in what way will it come?" Jesus said, "Have you uncovered the beginning, so that now you must seek the end? For in the place where the beginning is, the end will be also. Blessed is the one who stands in the beginning; that one will know the end and will not taste death".

Acknowledgements and Useful Information

Author website: www.simonsmall.info

Cover image: *Lost in Wonder* by Jane Small©
(jane-small.fineartamerica.com)

Organisations mentioned in the text

World Community for Christian Meditation: www.wccm.org
Centering Prayer: www.centeringprayer.com

Books about the contemplative life

Cave, Refectory, Road by Ian Adams (Liturgical Press 2012)

Living with Contradiction: An Introduction to Benedictine Spirituality
by Esther de Waal (Morehouse Publishing 1998)

A Book of Silence by Sarah Maitland (Granta Books 2009)

Books mentioned in the text

From the Bottom of the Pond: The Forgotten Art of Experiencing God in the Depths of the Present Moment by Simon Small
(O Books/Circle Books 2007)

Star Pilgrim: A Story of the Deepest Mysteries of Existence;
by Simon Small (O Books/Roundfire Books 2011)

The Invitation by Oriah Mountain Dreamer (Element Books 2003)

Mother Teresa: Come Be My Light by Brian Kolodiejchuk (Rider 2008)

Meister Eckhart: Selected Writings (Penguin Classics 1995)

Revelations of Divine Love by Julian of Norwich (Penguin Classics 1998)

Introduction to Metaphysics by Martin Heidegger (Yale Nota Bene 2000)

Coyote Waits by Tony Hillerman (HarperTorch 2009)

Two good books about the Gospel of Thomas

The Gospel of St Thomas by Marvin Meyer and Harold Bloom (HarperSanFrancisco 1993)

The Way of Thomas: Nine Insights for Enlightened Living from the Secret Sayings of Jesus
by John R Mabry (O Books 2007)

The brief quotes from the Gospel of Thomas scattered around the text are from John Mabry's thought-provoking book.

The Scripture quotations contained herein are from the New Revised Standard Version of the Bible, Anglicised Edition, Copyright © 1989, 1995 by the Division of Christian Education of the National Council of the Churches of Christ of the United States of America, and are used by permission. All rights reserved.

Printed in Great Britain
by Amazon